SKI BIDI OHIO RIZZ

THE GEN ALPHA & GEN Z DICTIONARY

TM DALIGGR

Skibidi Ohio Rizz
Copyright © 2025

ISBN
979-8-218-74188-4 (Paperback)

WELCOME

You likely have this book for one of three reasons:

1. You're old, and someone decided to prank you.
2. You're young, and someone is trying to tell you that they can't understand you.
3. You bought this for yourself, which is kind of weird.

Either way, this book is meant to educate the world about online Millennial, Gen Z, and Gen Alpha language. You will learn several definitions and then be put to the test via kindergarten exams and activities. Afterward, you'll be graded on your knowledge.

This book isn't meant to embarrass you, but you'll probably be embarrassed by the end--either because you know too little or you know too much.

Either way, sit back and have some humiliating fun.

HOW TO GRADE
How well do you know online lingo?

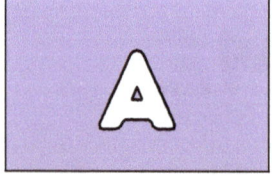 **A**   You did so well that you can't be a boomer.

 B   You know what? You know your stuff.

 **C**   Eh. It's possible you're a millennial.

 D   It's a miracle you know what technology is.

 F   The dinosaurs called. They miss you.

SPILLING BASIC PERIODT
THE TEA OHIO BOUJEE
GLOW UP SKIBIDI
DELULU LIT TOILET RIZZ
DOOM SCROLLING GYATT
BREAD YASSIFY SAVAGE
STAN MENTY B NO CAP
DELULU CRINGE SWAG
GOAT UNALIVE TROLL
SHADE FINESSE BASIC
CLAPBACK BOP SALTY
THIRST BOUJEE CLUTCH
TRAP ICONIC SIMP DRIP
SLAY RIZZ UNSERIOUS
NOOB SHOOK YASS SUS
SLAPS LOW KEYGASSED
HUMBLEBRAG GIGA CHAD
SIDE EYE OHIO DANK BOP

Rizz

[rizz] · noun

"Rizz" is a slang term that stands for "charisma"or "romantic appeal." Someone with "rizz" has a smooth, charming, and confident way of interacting with others, especially in romantic contexts.

Example: "Yeah, his rizz is insane. He gets so many dates."

What is chat ?

Chat

[chat] · noun

"Chat" refers to the real-time messages or comments that viewers post during a live broadcast. Streamers frequently address "Chat" by responding to viewer comments or engaging directly with their live audience.

Example: "Thanks for joining me for the live stream today, Chat! You're all great."

Glow up

[gloh-uhp] · noun

A "glow up" refers to a significant and noticeable improvement in someone's appearance, confidence, and overall well-being.

Example: "Tanner had the biggest glow up this year."

What is thirst trap ?

Thirst Trap

{thurst trap] · noun

"Thirst trap" is a slang term referring to a photo or video, often posted on social media, that is intended to attract attention and admiration, particularly for its physical appeal.

Example: "This is a total thirst trap edit."

What is lit ?

Lit

[Lit] · noun

"Lit" is a slang term that means exciting, excellent, or enjoyable. It is often used to describe a party, event, or experience that is particularly lively and fun. The term can also refer to someone being intoxicated.

Example: "That party was lit."

Sus

[suss] · noun

"Sus" is a slang term that stands for "suspicious" or "suspect." It is used to describe someone or something that seems untrustworthy, shady, or questionable.

Example: "Last night, Amy was acting a little sus during that game."

Mid

[mid] · noun

"Mid" is a slang term used to describe something that is mediocre, average, or just okay.

Example: "Eh, the food there was mid."

Cap

[kap] · noun

"Cap" is a slang term that means a lie or falsehood. When someone says "no cap," it means they are being truthful and not lying.

Example: "That's total cap. You were there yesterday."

Slay

[slay] · noun

"Slay" is a slang term used to describe someone doing something exceptionally well or looking fabulous.

Example: "The way Bella did that was a total slay."

Basic

[bay-sik] · noun

"Basic" is a slang term used to describe someone or something that is mainstream, unoriginal, or overly simplistic.

Example: "Not gonna lie, hun. That outfit is basic."

MATCHING

Match the characters to definitions

| CHAT | THIRST TRAP | LIT |
| RIZZ | GLOW UP | SUS |

1 [ ] Term that means exciting, excellent, or enjoyable.

2 [ ] A significant improvement in someone's appearance.

3 [ ] The name that streamers use to address their audience when live.

4 [ ] A photo/video that is intended to attract attention and admiration.

5 [ ] Slang that stands for "suspicious" or "suspect."

6 [ ] Having charisma or romantic appeal.

MATCHING

Match the characters to definitions

MID CAP	SLAY BASIC

7 | | An adjective meaning someone or something is unoriginal.

8 | | Describes someone doing something exceptionally well or looking fabulous.

9 | | A term that means a lie or falsehood.

10 | | Used to describe something that is mediocre, average, or just okay.

ANSWER KEY

How well did you do?

1 — **LIT** — Term that means exciting, excellent, or enjoyable.

2 — **GLOW UP** — A significant improvement in someone's appearance.

3 — **CHAT** — The name that streamers use to address their audience when live.

4 — **THIRST TRAP** — A photo/video that is intended to attract attention and admiration.

5 — **SUS** — Slang that stands for "suspicious" or "suspect."

6 — **RIZZ** — Having charisma or romantic appeal.

7 — **BASIC** — An adjective meaning someone or something is unoriginal.

8 — **SLAY** — Describes someone doing something exceptionally well or looking fabulous.

9 — **CAP** — A term that means a lie or falsehood.

10 — **MID** — Used to describe something that is mediocre, average, or just okay.

YOUR GRADE

Your final letter grade for this activity.

COMMENTS FROM THE PERSON
SCORING YOU:

17

Salty

[sawlt-tee] · noun

"Salty" is a slang term used to describe someone who is bitter, upset, or annoyed, usually over something minor or trivial. It implies that the person is being overly sensitive or reacting negatively to a situation that doesn't warrant such a strong response

Example: "Yeah, she was really salty about what happened at school."

Troll

[trohl] · noun

"Troll" refers to a person who deliberately provokes or annoys others online by posting disruptive comments online. The goal of a troll is often to elicit strong emotional responses or to derail a conversation. The term can also be used as a verb, as in "trolling."

Example: "He was trolling the live stream."

What is tea or spilling the tea ? 🔍

Spilling the tea

[spil-ing-thuh-tee] · noun

"Spilling the tea" means sharing gossip or revealing juicy, interesting, or scandalous information.

Example: "Alright, spill the tea. What happened yesterday?!"

What is Yeet?

Yeet

[Yeet] · noun

"Yeet" is a slang term that can be used in several ways, often to express excitement, energy, or enthusiasm.

Example: "That guy totally got yeeted during that game yesterday."

Noob

[noob] · noun

"Noob" is a slang term derived from "newbie," used to describe someone who is inexperienced or new to a particular activity, game, or community. It often carries a connotation of being clueless or lacking the skills and knowledge typical of more experienced participants

Example: "I'm such a noob at this game."

Boujee

[boo-zhee]· noun

"Boujee" (also spelled "bougie") is a slang term used to describe someone or something that is luxurious, fancy, or high-class, often in a way that is perceived as pretentious or trying too hard.

Example: "Cara is looking boujee today!"

Slaps

[slaps] · noun

"Slaps" is a slang term used to describe something, usually a song, that is really good, enjoyable, or hits hard in a positive way.

Example: "This food slaps. I'm obsessed!"

Clapback

[klap-bak] · noun

"Clap Back" is a slang term that refers to a sharp, witty, or assertive retort or comeback in response to criticism or an insult.

Example: "Yesterday, Eric was so rude to Tommy, but Tommy had the greatest clapback."

Bet

[bet] · noun

"Bet" is a slang term used to express agreement, affirmation, or approval, similar to saying "okay" or "sure." It can also be used to accept a challenge or to confirm that something will be done

Example: "You'll eat a rotten pickle? Bet."

Swag

[swag] · noun

"Swag" is a slang term that refers to a cool, confident, and stylish demeanor or appearance.

Example: He's got so much swag in that new outfit!

SPELLING

Fill in the blanks with the correct letters.

	sa__y
	t_ol_
	t_a
	y__t
	n_o_
	b_uj__

SPELLING

Fill in the blanks with the correct letters.

	sl___
	cl__ba__
	b_t
	s_a_

ANSWER KEY

Grade how well the tester did.

	salty		slaps
	troll		clap-back
	tea		bet
	yeet		swag
	noob		
	boujee		

YOUR GRADE

Your final letter grade for this activity.

What is menty b ?

Menty b

[men-tee-bee] · noun

"Menty B" is a slang abbreviation for "mental breakdown." It is used humorously or colloquially to describe a moment of overwhelming stress, anxiety, or emotional distress where someone feels they are losing control.

Example: "Millie is having a menty b right now."

Shook

[Shook] · noun

"Shook" is a slang term used to describe a state of being deeply surprised, shocked, or disturbed by something.

Example: "That movie was so scary. I'm shook."

What is stan ?

Stan

[stan] · noun

"Stan" is a slang term that means to strongly support, admire, or be a dedicated fan of someone or something.

Example: "I stan morally gray characters."

Bread

[bred] · noun

The slang word "bread" refers to money. It's often used to talk about earning, spending, or having money, similar to terms like "cash" or "dough."

Example: "Let's get this bread!"

What is Ship?

Ship

[Ship] · noun

"Ship" is a slang term derived from the word "relationship." It refers to the act of supporting or wanting two people, either real or fictional, to be in a romantic relationship.

Example: "I totally ship Alex and Amy."

Bop

[bop] · noun

"Bop" is a slang term used to describe a song that is very catchy and enjoyable.

Example: "This song is a total bop."

Ohio

[oh-hy-oh] · noun

"Ohio" has become a slang term often used in memes and internet culture to represent something weird, bizarre, or out of the ordinary.

Example: "That shirt is from Ohio, bro."

Serve

[surv] · noun

The slang word "serve" means to deliver something with style, confidence, or skill, often in the context of fashion, attitude, or performance.

Example: "Last night, she was serving in that dress."

What is wig ?

Wig

[wig] · noun

The slang word "wig" is used to express shock, amazement, or excitement, often in response to something impressive or unexpected. The term originates from the idea that something is so surprising or mind-blowing that it metaphorically makes your wig fly off.

Example: "Ok, you look amazing. Wig!"

Snatched

[snatch] · noun

The slang word "snatched" means looking incredibly stylish, attractive, or well-put-together. It's often used to compliment someone's appearance, particularly when their outfit, makeup, or overall look is exceptionally on point.

Example: "Her makeup is so snatched."

SENTENCES

Circle the correct word for each sentence.

Sheryl is having a total _____ right now. Like, a bad one.

Menty B   Shook

(circle the correct answer)

Wait, what?! That happened? Okay, I'm totally _____.

Ohio   Shook

(circle the correct answer)

The two of them are so cute together! I totally _____ it.

Stan   Ship

(circle the correct answer)

42

SENTENCES

Circle the correct word for each sentence.

He looked so good in those boots. It was a total _____.

Bop

Serve

(circle the correct answer)

Ok, this is so fun! I'm totally obsessed. _____!

Serve

Wig

(circle the correct answer)

Her eyeliner looks amazing. Her face is so _____.

Snatched

Bread

(circle the correct answer)

ANSWER KEY

Grade how well the tester did.

1. Sheryl is having a total _____ right now. Like, a bad one.

Menty B

2. Wait, what?! That happened? Okay, I'm totally _____.

Shook

3. The two of them are so cute together! I totally _____ it.

Ship

4. He looked so good in those boots. It was a total _____.

Serve

5. Ok, this is so fun! I'm totally obsessed. _____!

Wig!

6. Her eyeliner looks amazing. Her face is so _____.

Snatched

YOUR GRADE

Your final letter grade for this activity.

COMMENTS FROM THE PERSON
SCORING YOU:

Sus

[suss] · noun

"Sus" is a slang term that stands for "suspicious" or "suspect." It is used to describe someone or something that seems untrustworthy, shady, or questionable.

Example: "Last night, Amy was acting a little sus during that game."

What is no cap ?

No cap

[noh-kap] · noun

"No cap" is a slang term used to emphasize that someone is being truthful or honest. It's often used to assure others that what is being said is not an exaggeration or lie. Essentially, it means "no lie" or "for real."

Example: He said he's a pro gamer, but that's no cap!

What is delulu ?

Delulu

[di-loo-loo] · noun

"Delulu" is a slang term derived from "delusional." It is often used humorously or sarcastically to describe someone who is out of touch with reality or has unrealistic beliefs, particularly in the context of their fantasies or aspirations.

Example: She thinks she can become a pop star overnight—she's totally delulu!

Gyatt

[gyat] · noun

"Gyatt" is a slang term used to express strong excitement, surprise, or admiration, particularly when seeing someone attractive a playful exclamation, similar to saying "wow" or "oh my gosh." The term is often used in contexts where someone finds something or someone exceptionally attractive or impressive.

Example: That outfit is a gyatt moment for sure!

Ate

[ayt] · noun

The slang word "ate" is used to describe someone doing something exceptionally well, often with style and confidence. It's commonly used in contexts like performances, fashion, or any situation where someone excels.

Example: "She ate that performance."

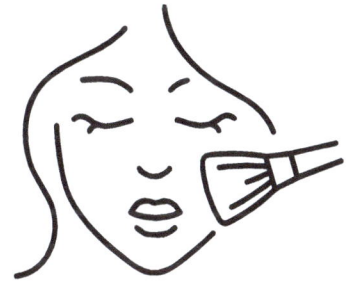

Yassify

[yas-si-fy] · noun

The slang word "yassify" refers to the act of dramatically enhancing or glamorizing someone or something, often using exaggerated makeup, filters, or editing techniques. The term originated from the combination of "yass" and "beautify."

Example: "She got totally yassified yesterday."

What is skibidi ?

Skibidi

[ski-bi-dee] · noun

A humorous, nonsensical word often used in the context of internet memes and gaming slang. It gained popularity through the "Skibidi Toilet" series on YouTube, where it is used in a playful and absurd manner, often associated with toilet humor and meme culture.

Example: After she made that joke, the whole room was in stitches—total skibidi moment!

What is sigma ?

Sigma

[Sig-muh] · noun

"Sigma" refers to a person, typically a man, who is independent, self-reliant, and operates outside traditional social hierarchies, excelling without seeking approval or following conventional paths.

Example: He's such a sigma, always doing his own thing.

What is fam ?

Fam

[fam] · noun

A slang term used to refer to friends or a group of close people who feel like family, often used to express camaraderie or affection in casual conversations.

Example: Can't wait to hang out with you this weekend, fam!

Yas

[yas] · noun

"Yas" is an enthusiastic slang term used to express strong approval, excitement, or support. It is often drawn out as "Yaaas" to convey even greater enthusiasm.

Example: She finally got the new iPhone—yas, that's amazing!

SPELLING

Have someone read the last ten words aloud and see if you can spell them correctly!

1. _____

2. _____

3. _____

4. _____

5. _____

Random Bonus Word:

_____

SPELLING

Have someone read the last ten words aloud and see if you can spell them correctly!

6. _____

7. _____

8. _____

9. _____

10. _____

Random Bonus Word:

_____

ANSWER KEY

Grade how well the tester did.

1. _DOOMSCROLL_
2. _NO CAP_
3. _DELULU_
4. _GYATT_
5. _ATE_
6. _YASSIFY_
7. _SKIBIDI_
8. _SIGMA_
9. _FAM_
10. _YAS OR YASSSSS_

YOUR GRADE

Your final letter grade for this activity.

COMMENTS FROM THE PERSON SCORING YOU:

Chad / Giga Chad

[giga-chad] · noun

The slang word "Chad" is often used to describe a stereotypical, confident, and conventionally attractive young man who is perceived as popular, assertive, and socially dominant. The term can be used both positively and negatively, depending on context.

Example: "Why is he being such a giga chad?"

Shade

[shade] · noun

"What is shade" can be used to describe indirect or subtle insults or criticisms. Throwing shade involves making a sly remark or gesture that points out someone's flaws or faults without being overtly aggressive.

Example: She threw some serious shade at the meeting with that comment.

Bruh

[bruh] · noun

"Bruh" is a slang term derived from "bro" or "brother," used informally to address or refer to a friend or acquaintance, often in a casual or humorous context. It is commonly used to express disbelief, frustration, or surprise.

Example: Bru, that was an amazing move you pulled off!

What is yikes or big yikes ?

Yikes

[word] · noun

"Yikes" is an expression used to show surprise, embarrassment, or concern, often in response to something awkward, shocking, or problematic.

Example: Yikes, I just realized I forgot to turn in my assignment!

GOAT

[goat] · noun

GOAT stands for "Greatest of All Time." It is used to refer to someone who is considered the best in a particular field or activity, often in sports, entertainment, or other competitive areas.

Example: That player is the GOAT of basketball—no one can match his skills!

What is side eye ?

Side eye

[side eye] · noun

"Side eye" refers to a subtle, sideways glance that expresses disapproval, skepticism, or suspicion without saying a word.

Example: When she heard the news, she gave him a serious side eye.

Him

{word} · noun

The slang word "him" is used to describe someone who is exceptionally confident, skilled, or dominant in a particular area, often implying that they are the best or most important person in that context. It's a way of saying someone is "the man" or the one to be reckoned with.

Example: "He IS him."

What is ghosting ?

Ghosting

[ghost-ing] · noun

"Ghosting" is a slang term that means to suddenly cut off all communication with someone, without any explanation. This can happen in various contexts, such as dating, friendships, or professional relationships, and involves ignoring calls, messages, and social media interactions.

Example: He was totally ghosting her after their last conversation.

What is bot ?

Bot

[bot] · noun

The slang word "bot" is used to describe someone who is perceived as behaving in a robotic, predictable, or unintelligent manner. It's commonly used in gaming and online communities to criticize players who seem to be making thoughtless or repetitive moves, similar to how a computer-controlled character (a bot) would behave.

Example: "Todd is playing like a bot right now."

Drip

[drip] · noun

"Drip" is a slang term used to describe someone's stylish or fashionable appearance, particularly their clothing and accessories. It implies a high level of fashion sense and confidence in one's look.

Example: His new outfit really has some serious drip!

TRACING

How steady is your penmanship?

GIGA CHAD

SHADE

BRUH

BIG YIKES

GOAT

SIDE EYE

TRACING

How steady is your penmanship?

HIM

GHOSTING

BOT

DRIP

BONUS TRACE

How steady is your penmanship?

LAST NIGHT, THERE
WAS THIS GIGA
CHAD BRUH. BIG
YIKES. BUT ALISON
WAS THERE, THE
GOAT. SHE GAVE
HIM THE SIDE EYE
AND THEN GHOSTED
HIM LATER. NO
SHADE, BUT
WITHOUT HER, IT
WOULD'VE BEEN
ROUGH.

YOUR GRADE

Your final letter grade for this activity.

73

What is unalive ?

Unalive

[un-uh-live] · noun

The slang word "unalive" is a euphemistic way of saying "dead" or "deceased" without using the more direct or harsh terms. It's often used on social media platforms and in online communities, particularly in contexts where using the word "dead" might trigger content moderation or where someone wants to discuss sensitive topics in a less distressing way.

Example: "Yeah, she unalived someone."

What is Savage?

Savage

[Sav-ij] · noun

"Savage" is a slang term used to describe someone who is bold, fearless, and unapologetically straightforward.

Example: "In the roasting session last night, Eric was a total savage."

High key

[high-kee] · noun

"High key" is a slang term used to emphasize something openly and without reservation. It means that someone is being straightforward, candid, and unafraid to express their feelings or opinions.

Example: I'm high key excited about the new game release next week!

What is low key ?

Low key

[Loh-kee] · noun

"Lowkey" is a slang term used to describe something that is modest, subtle, or not meant to attract attention. It can also mean slightly or somewhat, often used to express a desire to keep something discreet or not too obvious.

Example: I'm low key hoping it rains so we can have a cozy day indoors.

What is adulting ?

Adulting

[uh-dult-ing] · noun

The slang word "adulting" refers to the act of taking on responsibilities and tasks typically associated with being an adult, such as paying bills, doing household chores, managing finances, or making important decisions. It's often used humorously or ironically to describe mundane or challenging activities that come with adulthood.

Example: "I hated adulting today."

Periodt

[peer-ee-uhd- t] · noun

The slang word "periodt" is an emphatic way of saying "period," used to underscore a statement or opinion as final and not up for debate. The extra "t" at the end adds emphasis, signaling that there is nothing more to discuss.

Example: "I'm right. You're wrong. Periodt."

What is vibing or vibin' ?

Vibing

[Vy-bin] · noun

"Vibing" is a slang term that means enjoying the atmosphere or experiencing a good, relaxed, and positive state of mind.

Example: We're just vibin' at the beach, enjoying the sun and music.

Giving

[giv-ing] · noun

The slang word "giving" is used to describe when someone or something exudes a certain vibe, energy, or aesthetic, often with style or flair. It's usually followed by a description of what is being conveyed.

Examples: "He's giving 'tortured love interest.'"

What is flexin' or flexing ?

Flexin'

[fleks-in] · noun

"Flexin"is a slang term that refers to showing off or bragging, often about one's wealth, accomplishments, or physical appearance. It implies an attitude of confidence and pride in one's possessions or achievements.

Example: He was flexin' his new car at the party, showing it off to everyone.

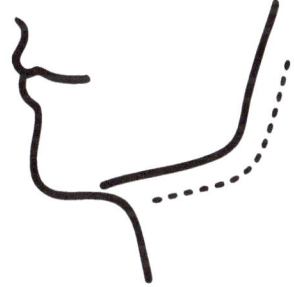

What is mewing ?

Mewing

[MYOO-ing] · noun

"Mewing" refers to a practice where people position their tongue against the roof of their mouth with the goal of improving jawline definition and facial structure over time.

Example: "Look at me. I'm totally mewing."

MULTIPLE CHOICE

Circle what you think is correct.

1. "Unalive" is a common censor or substitute for which word?

A. Vampire
B. Zombie
C. Murder

2. What does the slang term "savage" generally describe?

A. Weak
B. Bold
C. Calm

3. If someone says "I high key love tacos," they are...

A. Hungry
B. Obsessed
C. Indifferent

4. From the options below, which one most closely means "subtle"?

A. Low Key
B. Noob
C. Clutch

5. Which 80's slang term resembles "adulting" the most?

A. Handling business
B. On Point

MULTIPLE CHOICE

Circle what you think is correct.

6. What is the best synonym for "periodt" in slang usage?

A. For sure no	B. Maybe	C. Absolutely

7. What would be an appropriate response if someone says, "Your outfit is giving!"?

A. "Help?"	B. "Change."	C. "Thanks!"

8. In which year did Fortnite release their "Vibin'" season?

A. 2020	B. 2022	C. 2024

9. Mewing involves proper positioning of which body part?

A. Tongue	B. Eyes	C. Nose

10. Which 90's slang term resembles "flexin'" the most?

A. Tight	B. Putting on airs

ANSWER KEY

Grade how well the tester did.

1 "Unalive" is a common censor or substitute for which word? Answer: C. Murder

2 What does the slang term "savage" generally describe? Answer: A. Bold

3 If someone says "I high key love tacos," they are... Answer: B. Obsessed

4 From the options below, which one most closely means "subtle"? Answer: A. Low Key

5 Which 80's slang term resembles "adulting" the most? Answer: A. Handling Business

6 What is the best synonym for "periodt" in slang usage? Answer: C. Absolutely

7 An appropriate response to, "Your outfit is giving!"? Answer: C. "Thanks!"

8 In which year did Fortnite release their "Vibin'" season? Answer: B. 2022

9 Mewing involves proper positioning of which body part? Answer: A. Tongue

10 Which 90's slang term resembles "flexin'" the most? Answer: B. Putting' on Airs

YOUR GRADE

Your final letter grade for this activity.

COMMENTS FROM THE PERSON
SCORING YOU:

Clutch

[kluch] · noun

The slang word "clutch" is used to describe something or someone that comes through in a critical or high-pressure situation, often saving the day or making a significant impact. It's typically used to praise a timely or decisive action, like hitting a game-winning shot in sports or providing crucial help at the last minute.

Example: "He came in so clutch last game."

Clout

[klowt] · noun

"Clout" refers to influence, popularity, or social status, particularly on social media platforms.

Example: Her social media presence really gives her a lot of clout in the fashion industry.

What is mood ?

Mood

[mood] · noun

The slang word "mood" is used to express a feeling of strong relatability or agreement with something, often in response to a situation, image, or statement that perfectly captures a person's current emotions or vibe. It's like a shorthand way of saying, "I can totally relate to this" or "This is exactly how I feel."

Example: "See that garbage can? Mood."

Cringe

[krinj] · noun

"Cringe" is a slang term used to describe something that is awkward, embarrassing, or uncool.

Example: "Bro posted that TikTok and thought it was fire, but it was straight-up cringe.

Deadass

[Ded-ass] · noun

The slang word "deadass" is used to emphasize that someone is being completely serious or truthful. It's often used to convey sincerity, especially when something might be surprising or hard to believe.

Example: "I'm telling the truth. Deadass."

Simp

[simp] · noun

"Simp" is a slang term that refers to someone who is overly attentive, submissive, or fawning toward another person, often to the point of being perceived as excessively eager or desperate for their affection or approval.

Example: He's always doing extra things just to impress her; he's such a simp.

What is thicc ?

Thicc

[thik · noun

"Thicc" is a slang variation of "thick," often used to describe someone with a curvy, voluptuous body.

Example: She was rocking that outfit; it really accentuated how thicc she looked.

Gassed

[gast] · noun

The slang word "gassed" means feeling extremely excited, flattered, or confident, often as a result of praise or attention. It can also imply someone is overly confident or hyped up, sometimes to the point of being conceited.

Example: "Trish was so gassed about the concert."

What is hangry ?

Hangry

[hang-ree] · noun

The slang word "hangry" is a blend of "hungry" and "angry," used to describe the irritability or anger that some people feel when they are very hungry. It refers to the crankiness or bad mood that can arise when someone's blood sugar is low due to not eating, leading to impatience or short-tempered behavior.

Example: "Gerald was hangry today."

Finesse

[fi-nes] · noun

The slang word "finesse" refers to the ability to handle a situation or achieve something with skill, smoothness, and subtlety, often in a clever or crafty way. It can also mean to get what you want by being tactful, persuasive, or using charm.

Example: "Todd finessed that test."

WHAT RHYMES?

Circle the words that rhyme with each other.

	Clutch Bunch Such
	Pout Clout Coat
	Good Food Mood
	Cringe Range Tinge
	Dead Bead Red Ass Last Glass

WHAT RHYMES?

Circle the words that rhyme with each other.

	Sump	Skimp	Simp
	Flick	Thicc	Seek
	Passed	Guest	Gassed
	Hangry	Angry	Hardy
	Finesse	Guess	Fuss

ANSWER KEY
Grade how well the tester did.

	(Clutch)	Bunch	(Such)
	(Pout)	(Clout)	Coat
	Good	(Food)	(Mood)
	(Cringe)	Range	(Tinge)
	(Dead Ass)	Bread Last	(Red Glass)
	Sump	(Skimp)	(Simp)
	(Flick)	(Thicc)	Seek
	(Passed)	Guest	(Gassed)
	(Hangry)	(Angry)	Hardy
	(Finesse)	(Guess)	Fuss

YOUR GRADE

Your final letter grade for this activity.

COMMENTS FROM THE PERSON
SCORING YOU:

L

[EL] · noun

The slang word "L" stands for "loss" or "losing," and is often used to describe a situation where someone has failed, been defeated, or experienced something unfortunate. It can be used in various contexts, such as sports, games, or even daily life, to indicate that someone has taken a metaphorical "loss."

Example: "She took an L during the game."

W

[Dub-yoo] · noun

The slang word "W" stands for "win" or "winning," and is used to describe a situation where someone has succeeded, achieved something positive, or experienced a victory. It's often used to celebrate a success, whether big or small.

Example: "Last night's date was a W."

Sksksk

[sk-sk-sk] · noun

The slang term "sksksk" is an expression often used to convey excitement, laughter, or surprise, similar to "haha" or "lol." It's usually typed out as a string of letters that mimics the sound of someone stifling laughter or expressing excitement in a lighthearted way.

Example: "I'm dying right now. Sksksk."

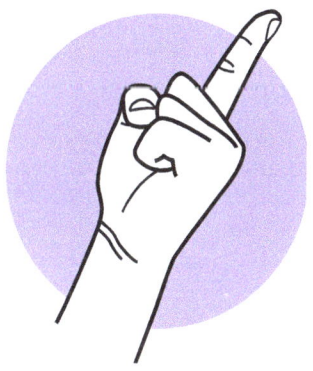

What is Karen ?

Karen

[kare-en]

The slang word "Karen" is a pejorative term used to describe a specific type of middle-aged woman who is perceived as entitled, demanding, or self-important. A "Karen" is typically characterized by behavior such as asking to speak to a manager over minor issues, displaying a sense of privilege, or being overly critical and judgmental.

Example: "Susan was such a Karen at the store."

Humblebrag

[Hum-bel-brag] · noun

The slang word "humblebrag" refers to the act of making a seemingly modest or self-deprecating statement that is actually intended to draw attention to something one is proud of or to subtly boast. It's a way of bragging under the guise of humility, often to avoid appearing arrogant.

Example: "That was a nice humblebrag, Erin."

ICONIC

Iconic

[eye-kon-ik] · noun

"Iconic" refers to something that is widely recognized and admired, often because it is representative of a particular style, era, or concept.

Example: Her style is so iconic that people immediately recognize her in any outfit.

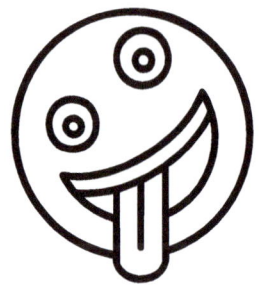

Unserious

{uhn-seer-ee-us] · noun

The slang word "unserious" is used to describe behavior, content, or situations that are intentionally humorous, light-hearted, or not meant to be taken seriously. It often characterizes a playful or carefree attitude, sometimes even in contexts where a serious demeanor might be expected.

Example: "OMG, you're being so unserious rn."

Dank

[dangk] · noun

"Dank" is a slang word that has evolved to mean something of high quality, particularly in the context of memes or cannabis.

- In memes: "Dank" refers to memes that are particularly humorous, clever, or high-quality.

Example: That meme you posted was really dank; it had everyone laughing out loud.

Bussin

[Bus-sin] · noun

"Bussin'" is a slang term that means something is exceptionally good, impressive, or exciting. It is often used to describe food that tastes delicious or experiences that are outstanding.

Example: That new song you played is bussin'; I can't stop listening to it.

What is situationship ?

Situationship

[Sit-you-a-shun-ship] · noun

A "situationship" is a term used to describe a romantic or involved relationship that is more than a casual fling but not quite a committed relationship.

Example: They decided to keep things casual and just enjoy their time together without defining it, so they ended up in a situationship.

SYLLABLES

Say the words out loud, count the syllables and color in the corresponding boxes.

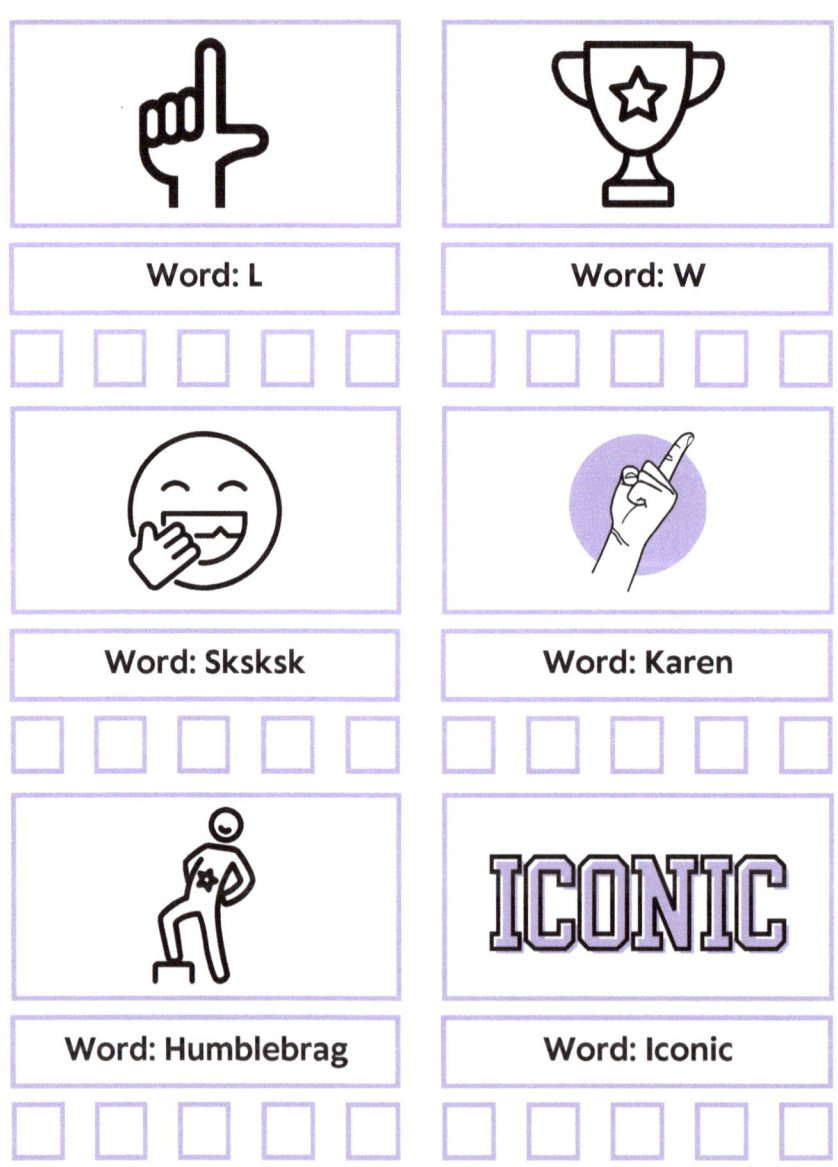

Word: L

Word: W

Word: Sksksk

Word: Karen

Word: Humblebrag

Word: Iconic

SYLLABLES

Say the words out loud, count the syllables
and color in the corresponding boxes.

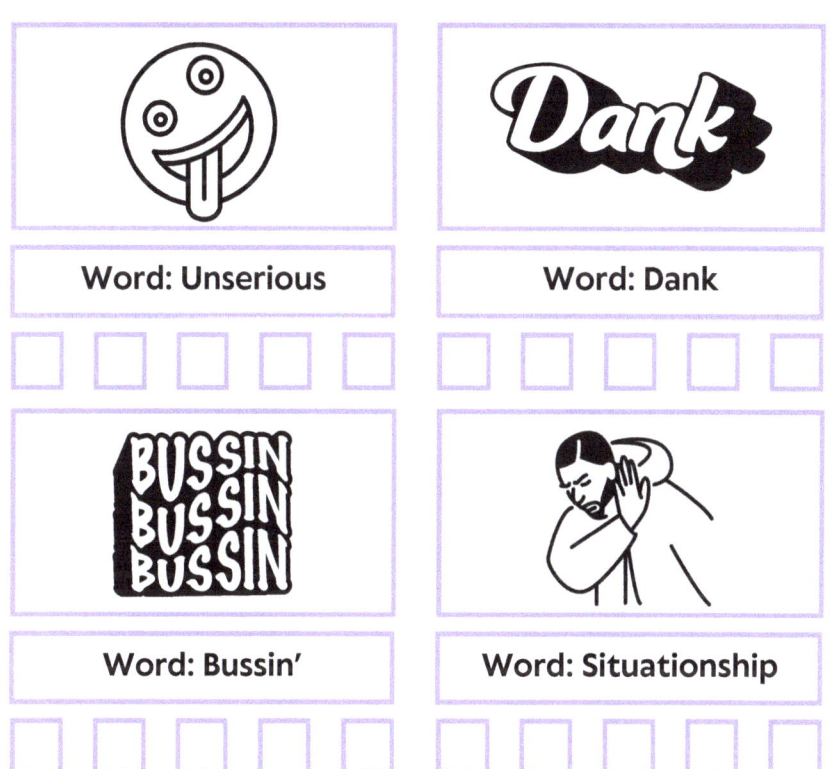

Word: Unserious

Word: Dank

Word: Bussin'

Word: Situationship

ANSWER KEY

Grade how well the tester did.

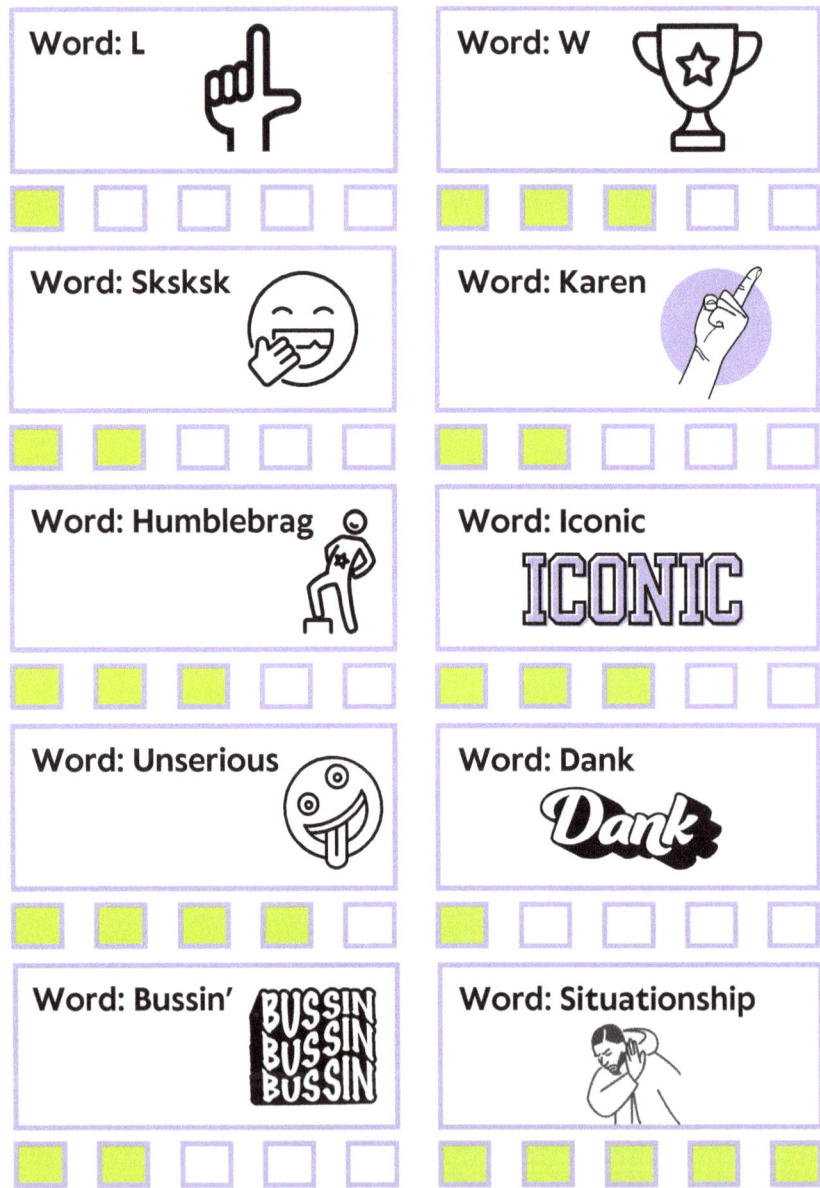

Word: L

Word: W

Word: Sksksk

Word: Karen

Word: Humblebrag

Word: Iconic

ICONIC

Word: Unserious

Word: Dank

Dank

Word: Bussin'

BUSSIN
BUSSIN
BUSSIN

Word: Situationship

YOUR GRADE

Your final letter grade for this activity.

What is Skibidi Ohio Toilet Rizz Bruh?

Skibidi Ohio Toilet Rizz Bruh

[ski-BID-ee oh-HI-oh TOY-let RIZ bruh] · noun

When combined, "Skibidi Ohio Toilet Rizz Bruh" is a playful, nonsensical phrase that mixes various internet slang elements to create a humorous, exaggerated, and slightly absurd expression. It might be used to describe something ridiculously funny, bizarre, and charming all at once.

Example: Skibidi Ohio Toilet Rizz Bruh!'

ANY WORDS WE MISSED?

Feel free to add more slang terms and definitions below!

ANY WORDS WE MISSED?

Feel free to add more slang terms and definitions below!

BONUS ROUND

EXTRA ACRONYMS + PHRASES

ACRONYMS

What does FOMO and BRB mean? Here are a list of common acronyms and their definitions.

ACRONYM	Stands for:	Definition:
FOMO	Fear of Missing Out	Anxiety that others might be having rewarding experiences without you.
IYKYK	If You Know, You Know	Information that's only understood by those who are in the know.
DIY	Do It Yourself	Creating or repairing yourself rather than hiring someone or buying an item.
ICYMI	In Case You Missed It	Highlights information or updates that someone might have not seen.
IMO	In My Opinion	Prefaces a statement that reflects the speaker's personal view or belief.
GRWM	Get Ready With Me	A video where someone shares their process of getting ready.
IMHO	In My Humble Opinion	Used to express a personal viewpoint, often with a modest, polite tone.
NOYB	None Of Your Business	Indicates that something is private or not for others to know about.
NPC	Non-Player Character	Describes someone who lacks independent thought or follows trends.
TFW	That Feeling When	An emotion or experience followed by an image, meme, or statement.
NVM	Nevermind	Indicates that something mentioned is no longer relevant or important.
AFAIK	As Far As I Know	Indicates the information is correct to the best of the speaker's knowledge.
TBH	To Be Honest	Used to preface a candid or straightforward statement
SMH	Shaking My Head	Used to express disappointment, disbelief, or frustration.
LOL	Laughing Out Loud	Shows amusement or that something is funny.
GOAT	Greatest Of All Time	Describes someone who is considered the best in a particular field.
AMA	Ask Me Anything	Invites others to ask questions, usually with the promise of honesty.

ACRONYMS

What does FOMO and BRB mean? Here are a list of common acronyms and their definitions.

ACRONYM	Stands for:	Definition:
DM	Direct Message	A private message between users on social media platforms.
IFYP	I Feel Your Pain	Expresses empathy for someone else's difficult situation or emotions.
FYP	For You Page	Refers to an algorithm-driven page, where personalized content is suggested.
SRSLY	Seriously	conveys that something is genuine or to express surprise or disbelief.
IRL	In Real Life	Differentiates what interactions occur in the physical world.
SOML	Story Of My Life	Means a situation is typical or reflects one's life experiences.
IDK	I Don't Know	Expresses uncertainty or ignorance.
AFK	Away From Keyboard	Indicates temporary unavailability online.
OC	Original Character	Means a unique creation, typically in fanfiction.
TMI	Too Much Information	Used when someone shares overly personal or unnecessary details.
TGIF	Thank God It's Friday	Expresses relief or excitement for the weekend.
RN	Right Now	Means something happening immediately or currently.
NGL	Not Gonna Lie	Used to introduce an honest or blunt statement.
HMU	Hit Me UP	Means to contact or message someone later.
WYD	What You Doing?	Asks someone what they're currently up to.
HBD	Happy Birthday	A quick and casual way to send birthday wishes.
WTF	What The F***?	Expresses surprise, disbelief, or confusion in situations.

ANY WORDS WE MISSED?

Feel free to add more slang terms and definitions below!

ANY WORDS WE MISSED?

Feel free to add more slang terms and definitions below!

PHRASES

These are unforgettable one-liners that you'll want to incorporate into your everyday life.

 **PHRASE:**
Standing on business

MEANS:
Confidently sticking to your principles or commitments, especially in challenging situations.

 **PHRASE:**
Throwing Hands

MEANS:
Engaging in a physical fight or confrontation.

 **PHRASE:**
Pick Me Girl

MEANS:
A girl who seeks attention or approval by acting differently, often by putting down other girls or trying to appear unique.

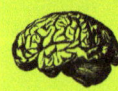 **PHRASE:**
Big Brain

MEANS:
Someone showing intelligence or clever thinking, often used humorously to praise smart ideas.

 **PHRASE:**
Let Him Cook

MEANS:
Giving someone the space to continue what they're doing, often implying they have a good idea or plan in progress.

 **PHRASE:**
Giving Me Life

MEANS:
Something is bringing you joy, excitement, or energy.

 PHRASE:
Living Rent Free

MEANS:
Something occupying your thoughts constantly, often without your control.

PHRASES

These are unforgettable one-liners that you'll want to incorporate into your everyday life.

 **PHRASE:** *Send It*

MEANS: *To go for something boldly or without hesitation, often used in daring situations.*

 **PHRASE:** *Girl Math*

MEANS: *The playful, sometimes illogical reasoning used to justify purchases or financial decisions.*

 **PHRASE:** *Millenial Pause*

MEANS: *The brief moment of hesitation or delay before starting to speak in a video, often associated with older generations.*

 **PHRASE:** *Left No Crumbs*

MEANS: *Doing something exceptionally well, with nothing left to criticize or improve.*

 **PHRASE:** *Give the 'Ick'*

MEANS: *Causing sudden feelings of dislike or repulsion, often in a romantic context.*

 PHRASE: *Vibe Check*

MEANS: *Assessing the mood, energy, or atmosphere of a situation or person.*

 **PHRASE:** *Fax, No Printer*

MEANS: *Something is undeniably true or accurate, with no need for further explanation.*

PHRASES

These are unforgettable one-liners that you'll want to incorporate into your everyday life.

 **PHRASE:** *Sleep On*

MEANS: *To underestimate or overlook something or someone's value or potential.*

 **PHRASE:** *Go Off*

MEANS: *To passionately express yourself or excel in something, often with enthusiasm or intensity.*

 PHRASE: *Caught in 4k*

MEANS: *Being caught doing something wrong or embarrassing with undeniable, clear evidence.*

 **PHRASE:** *Hit the Griddy*

MEANS: *Performing a popular dance move involving a playful, rhythmic walk with arm movements.*

 **PHRASE:** *Beige Flag*

MEANS: *A neutral or slightly odd trait in someone that isn't a dealbreaker but might raise mild curiosity or concern.*

 **PHRASE:** *Doing Me Dirty*

MEANS: *Betraying, mistreating, or unfairly taking advantage of someone.*

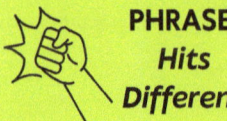 **PHRASE:** *Hits Different*

MEANS: *Something has a unique or more profound impact compared to usual experiences.*

PHRASES

These are unforgettable one-liners that you'll want to incorporate into your everyday life.

 **PHRASE:**
Pop
Off

MEANS:
To excel, stand out, or express something passionately, often in a bold or impressive way.

 **PHRASE:**
Throw
Shade

MEANS:
Subtly insult or criticize someone, often in a sly or indirect manner.

 PHRASE:
On
God

MEANS:
Affirming the truth or seriousness of a statement with strong conviction.

 **PHRASE:**
Nepo
Baby

MEANS:
Someone who benefits from family connections or privilege, particularly in gaining opportunities in certain industries.

 **PHRASE:**
Say
Less

MEANS:
You understand completely and no further explanation is needed.

 **PHRASE:**
It's [blank]
for me

MEANS:
Highlights a specific feature or behavior that stands out, usually in a relatable or humorous way.

 **PHRASE:**
On
Brand

MEANS:
Something aligns perfectly with someone's usual behavior, style, or identity.

PHRASES

These are unforgettable one-liners that you'll want to incorporate into your everyday life.

 **PHRASE:** *Struggle is real*

MEANS: *Acknowledges that a difficult situation or challenge is genuinely tough or relatable.*

 **PHRASE:** *Zero Chill*

MEANS: *Someone is being overly intense, dramatic, or lacking restraint.*

 **PHRASE:** *In my feels*

MEANS: *Being emotionally affected or deeply reflective, often about something personal.*

 **PHRASE:** *Left on read*

MEANS: *Someone saw your message but didn't respond, often implying disregard or disinterest.*

 PHRASE: *Secure the Bag*

MEANS: *Successfully achieving a goal, often related to making money or gaining something valuable.*

 **PHRASE:** *Doing the Most*

MEANS: *Going overboard or putting in excessive effort, often to the point of being unnecessary.*

 **PHRASE:** *Hot Girl Summer*

MEANS: *Confidently enjoying life, embracing fun, and focusing on self-empowerment during the summer.*

PHRASES

These are unforgettable one-liners that you'll want to incorporate into your everyday life.

 **PHRASE:**
5D
Chess

MEANS:
A complex, strategic move or plan that involves multiple layers of thinking, often beyond what others anticipate.

 **PHRASE:**
Adulting

MEANS:
Handling responsibilities and tasks associated with being an adult, often used humorously.

 **PHRASE:**
Bye,
Felicia

MEANS:
A dismissive way to say goodbye to someone you're not interested in or want to ignore.

 **PHRASE:**
Passenger
Princess

MEANS:
Relaxes in the passenger seat, enjoys the journey, gives directions, and brings the snacks.

 **PHRASE:**
Squad
Goals

MEANS:
The ideal or aspirational qualities of a group of friends or team.

 **PHRASE:**
Straight
Fire

MEANS:
Something is exceptionally good, impressive, or exciting.

 PHRASE:
Shoot Your
Shot

MEANS:
To take a chance or make an attempt, often in pursuing an opportunity or expressing interest.

PHRASES

These are unforgettable one-liners that you'll want to incorporate into your everyday life.

PHRASE:
Face Card

MEANS:
Always captivating, charming in every situation, and never loses their allure. "Her face card never declines."

PHRASE:
Sheeeeesh

MEANS:
An expression of disbelief or amazement, often used to react to something impressive or surprising.

PHRASE:
Victorian child

MEANS:
Overwhelming shock from modern life's unexpected sights and sounds. "Dubstep would put a Victorian child into a coma."

PHRASE:
Fr Fr

MEANS:
Short for 'for real, for real,' expressing genuine agreement or seriousness in a statement.

PHRASE:
-1000 Aura

MEANS:
Losing your coolness or confidence, becoming less impressive than before.

PHRASE:
Brain Rot(tting)

MEANS:
Slang for feeling mentally drained or dull from consuming too much low-quality content.

PHRASE:
Hot Take

MEANS:
A bold, controversial opinion shared confidently, often sparking debate or strong reactions.

ANY WORDS WE MISSED?

Feel free to add more slang terms and definitions below!

ANY WORDS WE MISSED?

Feel free to add more slang terms and definitions below!

THE END

Congratulations! You've made it to the end of the Gen Alpha and Gen Z Dictionary. You're either here because you skipped (cheater) or because you actually read every definition and did every activity (. . . weirdo).

Now, you officially know how to "slay" your modern day lingo and "throw shade" on those who can't. You're officially "big brained," as they say. Do you feel accomplished? You shouldn't.

Feel free to keep this book, so that it can put the unfortunate person who finds it in a coma (instead of a Victorian child).

CERTIFICATE

OF ACCOMPLISHMENT

This certificate is reluctantly awarded to:

_____

has successfully completed the Gen Alpha and Gen Z dictionary. Now, it's time to let them cook in the real world.

_____   _____
        Student   **Witness**
   (Please sign above)   (Please sign above)

CERTIFICATE

OF ACCOMPLISHMENT

This certificate is reluctantly awarded to:

_____

has successfully completed the Gen Alpha and Gen Z dictionary. Now, it's time to let them cook in the real world.

_____   _____
Student   **Witness**
(Please sign above)   (Please sign above)

CERTIFICATE

OF ACCOMPLISHMENT

This certificate is reluctantly awarded to:

_____

has successfully completed the Gen Alpha and Gen Z dictionary. Now, it's time to let them cook in the real world.

_____   _____
Student   **Witness**
(Please sign above)   (Please sign above)

CERTIFICATE

OF ACCOMPLISHMENT

This certificate is reluctantly awarded to:

_____

has successfully completed the Gen Alpha and Gen Z dictionary. Now, it's time to let them cook in the real world.

_____
Student
(Please sign above)

_____
Witness
(Please sign above)

IT'S TIME FOR YOUR GLOW UP!

Prove you have the ultimate rizz by making your own Lingo Dice.

ALPHA GEN
BINGO

Mark off how many slang terms you hear in a week!

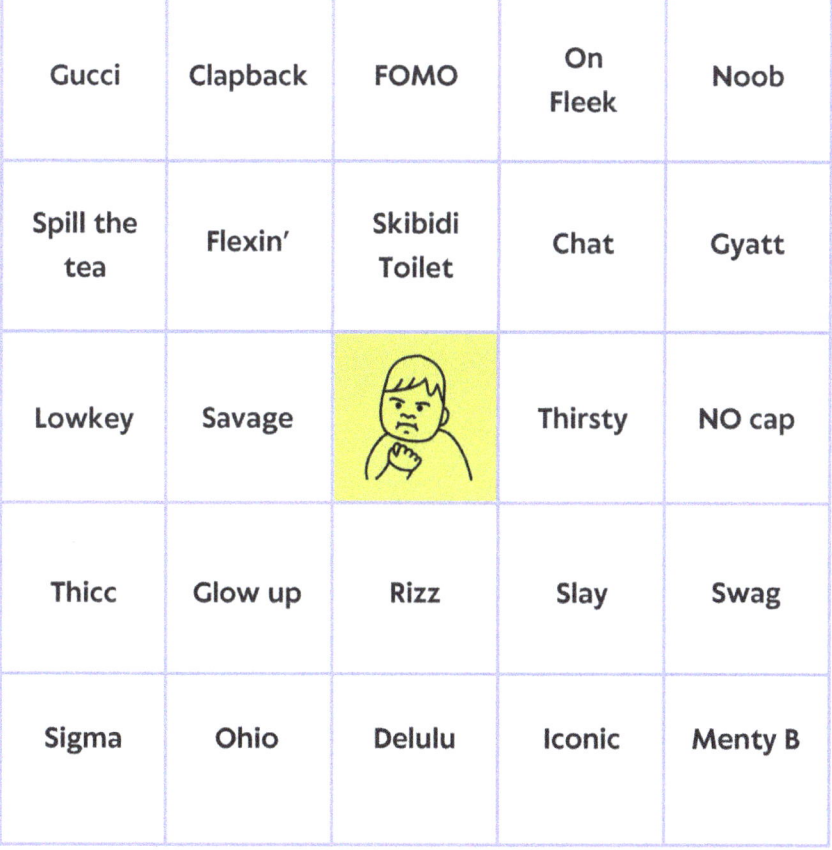

Gucci	Clapback	FOMO	On Fleek	Noob
Spill the tea	Flexin'	Skibidi Toilet	Chat	Gyatt
Lowkey	Savage		Thirsty	NO cap
Thicc	Glow up	Rizz	Slay	Swag
Sigma	Ohio	Delulu	Iconic	Menty B

www.ingramcontent.com/pod-product-compliance
Lightning Source LLC
Chambersburg PA
CBHW051318120626
46547CB00015B/2285